Earth in Silhouette
Poems
by
T. L. Cooper

ISBN: 978-1-943736-10-2

DEDICATION

Dedicated to the Earth who provides home for us all, those who
respect the Earth, and those working to keep the work
inhabitable for all beings.

Seeking Abundance

Traipsing through a meadow
Abundant with wildflowers
Blowing in the wind
Smashed beneath my feet
Wildlife sounds abundant
In the trees surrounding the meadow
I look toward the sky
Clouds float by, white and fluffy
Abundant against the bright blue sky
The sun's rays kissing my skin
Abundant with their warmth
Making my skin glow
There's nothing in my pockets
But an abundance of lint
Yet I feel richer than when
I hand over my credit card
To purchase a beautiful new....
Something, anything, nothing
To enhance my existence
Or at least proclaim to the world
The abundance in my life

Not My Land

This is not my land
Nor is it yours
We borrow it
From birth to death
Pretending it's ours
As we strip it of resources
With a sense of ungrateful entitlement
Greed dominating our interactions
Pretending like this ground we walk on
Can be owned by you or by me
Can be bought and sold
Fought over
Killed over
Our blood spilling across the world
In our desire for ever more ownership
Of an Earth that will never recognize
Our ownership
And an Earth that will revert to itself
As soon as it rids itself of us
All those false ownerships overgrown
With weeds and trees
Teeming with new life
To continue a cycle where
It proves over and over
That the land belongs to the Earth
Not to you and not to me
No matter what kind of constructs
We pretend control the land
We inhabit

Before Man

A time without man
Nature observes no borders
Life is free to roam

Nature to Love or Hate

Is it in a tree's nature
To love or to hate?
Is it in the soil's nature
To love or to hate?
Is it in the air's nature
To love or to hate?
Is it in water's nature
To love or to hate?
Is it in the sky's nature
To love or to hate?
Is it in the Earth's nature
To love or to hate?
We see love and hate
As natural states of being
Because we are human
And because our experience tells us
It's natural to love and it's natural to hate
But what if it isn't?
What if love and hate are constructs
Humans created to further this agenda or that agenda?
What if the only thing in our nature is to survive
And all the rest is just window dressing
To inflate our sense of superiority
Over the trees that provide us oxygen
Over the soil that provides nourishment to the plants we eat
Over the air that provides us the breath we breathe
Over the sky that brings us light by day and dark by night
Over the Earth that provides us a home
What if love and hate are as fleeting as the moment we exist?

A Few Things That Matter

A cool breeze on a sunny day
Rain in the middle of a drought
Snakes in the grass
Trees in the forest
Oxygen to breathe
Compassion for one another
A kitten's sweet purr
A dog's wagging tail
Clean water to drink
Pure air to breathe
Nutritious food to eat
Icecaps being frozen
Bees and butterflies to pollinate food
Diversity in the world
Honesty in our interactions
Generosity toward one another
The sun and the moon
The planet on which we live
Understanding each other
Equality
Unity
Love

Sunrise Walk

Light arises from dark
Stream gurgles welcome to day
Trees glisten with dew

On Top of Your Home

I walk into your home
Build a house over your home
Wonder why you invade my house
Built on top of your home
See you slither through my yard
On the property I bought
Watch you eat my plants
From the safety of my house
Built on top of your home
You scurry up the tree I planted
To replace the trees I felled
When I built my house
On top of your home
Do you think I invaded
Do you think I stole
Do you think I colonized
When I bought the land
On which your home existed
In the trees, the forest, the meadows
Though I might claim to own this land
And hold a deed that proclaims my ownership
You'll just eat that piece of paper
Without stopping to consider its value
In this world where we pretend we own
The land you inhabited long before humans
Do you look at us and think us silly
With all our trapping of success
As you move away from the house
I built on top of your home

Springs's Renewal

Bare branches
Tiny buds
Renewal awaits
Blooms prepare to burst forth
Sparking imagination
Beauty anticipated
Delicate flowers dance in the wind
Bare hearts
Tiny buds of compassion
Renewal awaits
Love prepares to burst forth
Sparking imagination
Beauty anticipated
Delicate emotions dance in the wind
The cold winter passes
Renewal awaits
Heartache finds a fresh start
In the warming sun
In the thawing earth
White bark of a birch tree
Glows against fresh greenery
The purity of possibility
Letting go of pain
To welcome happiness
Renewal awaits
Those willing to embrace
Spring

Bees Buzz

The bees buzz
Through the air
Moving trucks for nectar
Creating flowers and fruit
They tell each other
Beware that plant
It killed my friend
Buzz, buzz, buzz
Mine, too
Buzz, buzz, buzz
Avoid this plant and that
The nectar killed
Whole colonies
Nectar turned poison
The bees buzz on
Doing the job they
Evolved to do
Spreading nectar
Creating food for humans
With no need for compensation
With no need for recognition
With no need for glorification
They do their job
Day after day
Year after year
Decade after decade
Century after century
Millennia after millennia
The bees buzz on
Feeding the world
Strategizing their own survival

In a world that seems intent
On killing them
Perhaps they'll figure out a way
To grow super strong stingers
With their own super strong poison
To protect their lives
They'll buzz on
Starving us by not spreading nectar
Buzz, buzz, buzz
Trying to send us all a message
If we want to survive
We need to understand
Just how connected we all our
Will we listen to the bees
As they
Buzz, buzz, buzz
Past our ears
Searching for nectar
That is not yet compromised
By human interference
The stories the bees must tell
Trying to figure out why
Humans are so suicidal
All in the name of greed
Buzz, buzz, buzz...

Wildflowers and Weeds

The grass tickled my ankles
But it felt more like an itch
An itch driving me to step high
Move away from the moment
I wanted to embrace
Like so many other times
When I found myself walking
In a field of wildflowers and weeds
Unable to discern which was which
Seeing the moment as something
Undecipherable
Wondering if I could have
Wildflowers without weeds
Thorns scratching my calves
My blood joining the Earth
Ready to feed both
Wildflowers and weeds
This small cut there
And another here
A thorn stuck in my skin
All those moments I cherished
Turned to weeds thriving in the midst
Of a meadow of dying flowers
As I strolled along looking for
Wildflowers strong enough to withstand
The onslaught of weeds in their midst
Then I saw the perfect wildflower
All its blooms sparkling in the sun
Like a smile beckoning me forth
Like eyes promising me a future
Like a tongue teasing me with pleasure

I ran toward that perfect bloom
Risking the burrs and the thorns
Cutting, scraping, leaving rashes
I tripped over rocks
And caught my foot in holes
Stumbling, bumbling, crumbling
Toward that perfect bloom
Just out of reach
Blowing in a perfect wind
On a perfectly sunny day
I fell into a mud puddle
Soaking my knees
Still, I ran forward
Dirty and lost and determined
As the clouds rolled in
Hiding the sun
Opening to soak my hair and my skin
Still, I ran toward the perfect
Wildflower in the midst of weeds
Knowing if I could reach it
Everything would change
I watched all the other wildflowers
Crumple beneath my careless feet
Racing toward the perfection I desired
A roll of thunder, a flash of lightning
Still, I couldn't stop running
I'd risk it all for the perfect
Wildflower growing in the weeds

But, the wildflower only laughed at me

Earth

Surrounded but alone
Embraced but not secure
Loved but not respected
Needed yet abused
Giving but unappreciated
Beautiful yet dying
Peaceful yet destructive
Vengeful or self-protective
Providing yet not replenished
Majestic but humble
Stable though turbulent
Progressive yet traditional
Diverse but the same
Ever-changing yet reliable
Home
Life
Lover
Killer
Provider
Mother
Father
Contradictory
Our Earth

Previously appeared in the anthology Standing: Poetry by Idaho Women 2005 and on Associated Content

Grapes

Grapes hang on a vine
Green, red, awaiting picking
Ready to delight

Around the World

Floating weightlessly
Floating effortlessly
Across the world
On ancient dust particles
Swirling through the air
The Sahara feeding the Amazon
Weightlessly, effortlessly
On sediment from the Amazon floor
Flowing through rivers to the sea
Feeding plankton
Weightlessly, effortlessly
On lightning lighting up the sky
Splitting nitrogen atoms
Forming nitrogen oxide
Feeding plants nitrites
Weightlessly, effortlessly
Hot and cold colliding
At Antarctica
Completing the cycle
So it can begin again
Forever ongoing
Forever supporting life
Until a cog in the system
Exploits the process
Pushing for its own agenda
Turning that which should be
Weightless, effortless
Into a challenge for survival
Destroying in the name of progress
Forgetting that for every exhale
Floating around the world

Weightless, effortless
On the processes that keep the world turning
An inhale must be taken
Completing the cycle

Travel

I've traveled by plane
I've traveled by car
I've traveled by train
Riding the highways
Flying above
Mountains and meadows
Farms and cities
Meeting people
A short laugh
An anecdote
A debate
Connections made
Experience expanded
Traveling the world
Buses, subways, taxis
Exposing the world
I've watched faces
So familiar and so different
Not really seeing one another
Racing past one another
Intent on the next task
All of us together and yet not
How much we share
How much we hide
How much we pretend
Trying to be seen
Trying to be unseen
Striving to create
A world of connections
Without risking too much
Such a contradiction we live

In this world where we can
Travel so far so fast
And yet we refuse to embrace
All that makes the world worth seeing

Orchid Wide

Orchids blow in air
White against the stormy sky
Window open wide

The Earth

Everyday should be Earth Day
Without the Earth
We cease to exist
We may dream of floating above the clouds
But we must always come back to Earth
We forget to notice
The beauty nature offers us
We think somehow
The Earth owes us
When in fact it gives us everything
Including our very lives
In return we strip it of
The very things that sustain us
Today, every day...
We should take a moment
To remember
Without the Earth
Without the air
Without the soil
Without the plants
Without the trees
Without the animals
Without the water
There would be no
Us
To inhabit the Earth

Imprint

Offer me something new
Instead of what we've already been
Show me where we can go
Guided by the stars on a dark night
Along a seaside path
Where our footprints are erased
Before they can impact the earth
Proving we only have a moment
Before our existence disappears
Taking with it all our infinite possibility
As we continue to walk along
Oblivious to what we leave behind
Refusing to stand still long enough
To imprint our truth even on ourselves
As we rush forward into what comes next
Never appreciating the steps
Washed away by the tides

What the Earth

You there
On the other side of
The Earth
Do you wonder about me
On your other side of
The Earth
Each of us seeking for
Our needs to be met
The needs that match
And the needs that differ
We stand on opposite sides of
The Earth
Looking to the sky
Clouds, rain, sun, wind
Looking to the ground
Soil, sand, clay, dirt
Looking to the waterways
Rivers, lakes, oceans, creeks
Looking for the answers
To feed our bodies
To feed our souls
To feed our hearts
Reaching for the connection
That brings us closer to understanding
Each other's needs
Even as we destroy each other's needs
And often our own in pursuit of gain
But what do we gain when we
Plunder the very lifegiver
We call home
Meeting today's needs

At the expense of tomorrow
Someday the Earth's bill
Will come due
And we'll be left standing
With only the deficit in hand

Icy Branch

Holding the balance
Between the past and future
On an icy branch

Beauty in Destruction

Waves lick my feet
As I walk along
The deserted beach
Not a living being in sight
Looking out over the waves
Moving in a rhythm that
Plays a symphony in my head
A soft lullaby
A dance beat
A romantic waltz
An angry headbanger scream
All muddled together
I look around searching for
Someone to join me in this
Journey to save what's left
The ocean reminding me
The Earth will have its way
With or without me
In the distance I see
Someone unlike me
Waving me forward
We reach one another
Begin to speak
Languages foreign to our ears
Soon we manage to communicate
Our dismay at all that's been lost
Destroyed by our greed and indifference
Grasping hands, arms, we embrace
Determined to rebuild what we can
Looking for others
Somehow all those differences

That once divided us have disappeared
We have only us to make things right
Hatred will only get in the way
So we find a way to cooperate
And discover we always had
More in common than the world
Would have had us believe

So I ask you now
Will it take our destruction for us
To find the beauty in each other?

Outstretched Hand

I walked among the trees
The leaves dripping with rain
Heavy on the branches
Weighted down
I ducked my head under
This branch and that one
Stepped around puddles of water
Slid my foot over the pebbles
Seeking the sensation of movement
Along the path where we once stood
Hand in hand looking for a place to sneak a kiss
The sun above us shining through these same trees
Now dripping wet
Laughter escaped my lips as a large drop
Landed smack on the top of my head
My clothes soaked through
My hair matted to my neck
I remembered you telling me
Nothing would ever change between us
As the clouds moved across the sun
I knew your words were only wishful thinking
This forest, you, me, the world
They all change
Love and hate in a constant battle
For all the potential we hold inside
Afraid to show the world
Who might take advantage of us
To feed the greed that propels divisiveness
I feel the heat on my face
Open my eyes to a burned-out forest
Ash floating through the air

The leaves heavy with rainwater
Completely bare and blackened
The soil beneath my feet dry as a desert floor
You changed
I changed
We changed
The world changed
Love changed
Hate changed
Leaving behind only
Destruction and despair
Yet, as I stood in the wasteland
That used to be a lush forest
I heard the gentle sound of birds singing
Somewhere off in the distant
And for that moment
All the change before me vanished again
And I saw hope as I imagined
New growth sprouting forth
From you and me and the Earth
And I reached out my hand
Offering to walk hand in hand
Once again
Maybe someday you'll reach back
And hope will manifest something
We can use to rebuild
All that's been destroyed
So I'll stand here as long as I can
With my hand outstretched
Waiting to feel yours clasp mine

Best Case Earth

Your hand in mine
Walking along
Silence, comfortable and sweet
Connecting us
As we move forward together
Into new adventures
Hills and streams
Mountains and valleys
Oceans and deserts
Fixing what's before us
Restoring what once was
Together seeing what can be
With a little generosity and love
Trees blooming
Streams clean enough to drink
Food that nourishes
Air that fills lungs with life
Removing the destruction
Wrought by those who only value
The green of money
And see the green of Earth
With dollar signs in their eyes
Best case scenario
We correct enough for
A new generation to have a chance
To finish what we started
So the future won't end
Quite so soon

Stormy Day

(a san san)

Leaves dance on the wild wind
Clinging to staid trees
In spite of the brewing storm
Pushing toward day's end
Where sunset frees
The storm's raging clouds
To beat rain upon trees in a swarm
To silence leaves in wet shrouds

Whale Mom and Child

I watched as the sea rose
The whale drifting with it
Spewing water from its blowhole
Surrounded by an island of debris
Slowly pushing it this way and that
As the wind whipped the bits of plastic
Up and down destroying the home
Of the whale holding its baby close
For fear of the damage human beings inflict
In the name of greed
The most selfish of the lot is the human
Who sees the whale, the dolphin, the shark, the swordfish
And thinks of only how to exploit them
I watched as mother and child whale navigated
Through the debris humans threw away cavalierly
How does a whale mom explain this trashing of their home?
How do we?

Only Home

On this ride
Around the sun
Seeing yesterday reflected
In the moon
Secrets whispered into the dark night
Traveling to the stars
Where they collide with wishes
People standing here
People standing there
We all bask under the same sun
We all stare up into the moon's reflection
We all feel the heat of the sun
Yet we pick a fight over territory, belief, words
Fight to the death
Killing those so like us that we deem different
For the sake of having an enemy
As if having a foe somehow gives us purpose
But, what if, just what if
We got it all wrong
What if our purpose
Isn't to accumulate, to acquire, to conquer
What if our purpose
Is to love, to give, to unite
As you stand there
And I stand here
We both count the stars
Lighting up the sky
With light that travelled
Longer than humanity has existed
To light up our dark sky
And yet we stand toe to toe

Ready to kill each other
Over the only home
We'll ever know

Across the Earth

Soil, water, air, fire
Play in the space
We call Earth
Working together
To give us life
The very life
We rip apart
Devalue, destroy
At whim
Using the very elements
The Earth provides us
To survive
Taking the positive
And turning it on its head
Until the negative is all that's left
That which builds destroys
That which destroys builds
It all depends on whose hands
Control the elements
And what power they wish to wield
Mixing and blending the elements
Earth gives us to create
In ways that do nothing but destroy
Until one day there's nothing left of us
The Earth has the last laugh
Gathering back her elements
For the next evolution
Maybe someday a species will evolve
That builds more than it destroys

Quartziferous Lives

Mining the quartz
From the depths of the Earth
Ripping the world to shreds
So we can have beauty
In our kitchens and bathrooms
Bringing the outdoors in
Calling it modern
In spite of the millions of years
It took to form
But, oh, we need to have that
Quartziferous material adorning
Our homes as status symbols
To prove we lead
Quartziferous lives

Overlit

Streetlight on the sidewalk
Blotting out
Moonlight above
Starlight twinkling
The dark night interrupted
By the artificial light
We created to prolong our days
To work more hours
To play more hours
To trick night into believing it's day
Oh, the things we do to manipulate
The world to our will
Regardless of the cost
All because we want what we want
We exploit the resources around us
We manipulate nature's order
We destroy the atmosphere
All in the name of progress
As we take more than we give
We speed along not only our demise
But the demise of all living things
The demise of the Earth itself
And, yet, we value money
Far more than our home

Swollen Waterways

The swollen river
Spills over the banks
Flooding streets
Rapids pulling us all under
Drowning us in a tempest
We can't outrun
As the oceans rise
And the plains turn to deserts
The sun melts icy mountaintops
The glaciers break apart
Floating like boats
Taking frozen toxins
Along for the ride
To deposit on distant shores
Where they meet up with discarded plastic
Buildings, old and new, lost to swollen shores
Bruised and battered shorelines losing their appeal
Until the moment is forgotten
Life resumes with rebuilt cities awaiting
The next deluge, wondering if that will be the one
That swells and never recedes

Murder Weapon: Bottle Cap

Do you ever stop to think
Do you ever stop to consider
What happens to that piece of plastic
You tossed on the ground and kicked into the river
As it travels down the river, rolling over in the dirt
Mistaken for food
Finding its way into the belly of a turtle
Indigestible…
Joining other pieces of plastic
Until the turtle dies a torturous death
Releasing the plastic pieces
To travel to the ocean
To be eaten by birds, whales, dolphins
That tiny piece of plastic
Killing indiscriminately
Time and again
As the minutes turn to hours
As the hours turn to days
As the days turn to months
As the months turn to years
As the years turn to decades
Still recognizable
As the bottle top you dropped
Without a second thought
To be a murder weapon
And there it is
Come back to haunt you
On the beach where
You pick up the bottle cap
Carelessly dropped by
Someone else

Or maybe it was yours…
How could you know?

Black Bile

The black bile
Of melancholy
Seeped from my pores
Covered my body in its
Cancerous destruction
Overtaking all the blood and sweat
I poured out in my struggle
To float above the clouds
To avoid the storms of the angry gods
Set on destroying the sun and the moon
And the beautiful harvests we planted in spring
As we fought to nourish this new beginning
Planted on soil depleted of all its nutrients
Leaving behind only the blackness of hate
To destroy every bit of love and compassion
With the judgment of the unjust
Raining down injustice on the just
Thickening black bile depressing
The civilization we so steadfastly obliterated
In the name of destiny and self-righteousness
Oh, yes, the black bile we spread around the globe
To destroy anyone who didn't submit to our will
And often even those who did
So I searched the sky for the face of a goddess or two
Wondering if I'd find more equality in a goddess than a god
Only to find my way back to the Earth where I'd left
The black bile spread by the followers of the gods and goddesses
Blamed and worshipped with equal measure
For the actions of those followers
Who never wanted to take responsibility for the black bile spreading
Across the world

Creating a melancholy none of us will escape alive
As the Earth seeks to rid herself of the cancer killing her
A black bile so sad in its approach it can't even see
It's committing suicide

Blackberry Bush

The sweetest blackberry
Nestled between the sharpest thorns
Tempting my fingers to risk the bloody prick
To feel the juice dripping over my tongue
The sweet nectar sliding down my throat
I stare at the thorns
I stare at the blackberry
Large and glistening in the light
My finger trembles as I reach for it
The leaves rustling in the wind
The white blooms floating away
As a new berry bursts forth
Green turning to pink
Before turning to a
Rich, juicy purple berry
Nestled between thorns
Tempting me all over again
Making me forget the last time
The thorns pricked my finger
As I picked the berry
Risking the pain for the pleasure
Of a beautifully plump sweet blackberry
Hanging on the blackberry bush
Protecting its fruit from me

Sun Symbols

Sun kissed the treetop
Shining through the branches
Illuminating the needles
Reminding me of that fake plastic star
We placed on top of the Christmas tree
When I was a child
We plugged it in to shine
But as I stood and stared at
The real sun shining through the needles
All the false yesterdays suddenly felt lit
On fire
Unable to hide
Those moments we pretended
All those symbols meant something
Until the day they were smashed to bits
Little left of childhood memories
Crumbs of symbols that could disappear in an instant
Yet the sun will return to
Highlight that evergreen day after day
Season after season
Until the tree is no more
While all those precious plastic symbols
Pollute the ground where they lost their meaning
I tried to capture the sun glowing through the treetop
In a photograph
But even that becomes only a symbol
Standing in for the real thing

Damage is Done

When the damage is done
What's left to do?
Forests become deserts
Deserts become seas
The land shifts
Mountains collapse
Hills rise
Heat scorches
Habitats lost
Food supplies decimated
Water evaporates
Stumbling along
Paying little attention
Grasping for the latest technology
In search of connection
While whole species go extinct
All in the name of greed and power
Money driving the world into ruin
Accumulating possessions to increase self-worth
To prove to the world there's more than there is
Becoming ever more devoid of compassion
Valuing profits over people
Watching the bottom line rise
Alongside the sea levels
Racing against the destruction both wreak
Artificial success riding waves of despair
In search of happiness escaping the atmosphere
All the while pretending some savior is coming
To hit a reset button that will create a paradise
From the remains left in the wake of the unacknowledged loss

Ice Covered Core

Twig coated in ice
Radiating in the sun
Unveiling the core

Future Flow

Flowing toward tomorrow
On white water rapids
The freezing water
Dirtied by the refuse dumped
Into its rising waters
Taking it across borders
The flowing water doesn't care exists
Dumping its toxins into the flooded fields
Where food no longer grows to feed
The desolate towns along the way
The sun baking the boulders of hope
Trying to hold back the destruction
As pools of plastic clog the confluence
Of river and ocean
The flow of the present stopped by the past
Destroying the future
All for the sake of keeping the money flowing
From one greedy hand to another and back again

Mother Clock

I looked at the clock
Another second slid by
Another minute ticked by
Another hour wasted
Another day gone
This division between us
Grows no closer to closing
As we live lives on the surface
Of an Earth we're destroying
At neck break speed
The artifice of time
Telling us to hurry up
And that we have time
All in one breath
I turned from the clock
Refusing to watch
Time pass
Outside the sun rose
The sun traveled across the sky
The sun set
Trees bloomed
Trees changed colors
Trees lost their leaves
Time passes
Whether I looked at the clock or not
The ice caps melted
The snow came
The oceans rose
The hurricanes battered coasts
The volcanoes erupted
Lives were lost

Homes destroyed
The sun rose
The sun travelled across the sky
The sun set
Time passed
I looked back at the clock
I waited too long...
The clock stopped
It was too late...

Your Nature

Is this your nature?
I wonder as I watch you
Destroy the natural world
Plundering all the glorious nature
That provides us a home
That offers us nutrients
That allows us to thrive
Our survival depends on
The very nature you destroy
And yet it seems to come
So naturally to you
As I scream into the void
Because my nature says
Protecting nature benefits us all
While you ask how you can
Exploit nature to fill your coffers
While we all strive to avoid
Our coffins
And yet you smile as you find
Yet another way to destroy
Yet another thing we need
Ignoring all the warning signs
All around us
But it is in Earth's nature
To survive
Even as we drive our own species
To extinction

Shovel

The shovel slid through the dirt
The grass parted ways leaving
A cut too jagged to be surgical
But strategic nonetheless
Separating the roots from the blades
The roots will survive; the blades will die
It's inevitable unless...
The shovel pushed through the roots
Until nothing was left was a large, empty hole
Waiting to be filled with something brand new
Perhaps something more amenable to the climate

Most Arrogant Animal

Roaming the Earth
Arrogant in inferiority
Falsely believing in their superiority
Never stopping to see
Their place in the hierarchy of nature
Placing themselves above all others
Thinking everything is made to serve them
Destroying everything in their path
In the name of progress
Ravaging nature to fuel their greed
Killing any other being that gets in their way
Without a second thought
All the while claiming they are the civilized ones
The only civilized ones
Leaving death and destruction in their wake
For the next generation to clean up
Because their selfishness is all that matters
In a world where immediate gratification
Rules everything else
The most arrogant animal of them all
Has long forgotten they're just another animal
Inhabiting an Earth with many other animals
Who have a right to their homes
Who have a right to resources
Who have a right to survive
But when you're the most arrogant animal
You tend to think it was all created
Just for you

Still Blue Lake

Stillness, deep and dark
Reflection repelling touch
Unbroken blue lake

Urban Farm

We dug up the yard
Planted tomatoes, cucumbers, peppers
Watered them religiously
Added fruit trees
Apple, peach, fig, cherry
Watered them religiously
The herbs holding on
Mint, oregano, thyme
Even when we forgot to water them
Made a compost box
To feed our food
With our food
Created our own little farm
Right there in the city
Seemed like it was easier
To grow a garden
In the country
But maybe that's my memory
Romanticizing work shared by family
The sweet nectar of a fresh tomato
Tasted so different grown in the Kentucky soil
Than the Idaho soil
Than the Oregon soil
How could that be?
My urban garden
My urban farm
Never measuring up
To the memories
Of the land
I abandoned
In search of

A future so different

Flames Lick the Sky

Flames lick higher
Destroying everything in its path
Turning trees to ashes
Evaporating waterfalls
Charring brush
Moving faster than a racehorse
Scorching the earth
Snowing ashes for miles
Filling the air with poison
Sucking oxygen from the air
Silencing the birds
Rushing forth like a hurricane
Blowing in to flood the world
Killing everything in its path
The earth seeking revenge
For human beings' undeniable
Greed, apathy, and carelessness
Burning it all to the ground
So nature can rise up again
Stronger than ever
Changing the world
Erasing the constructs of destruction
Without hesitation
So many chances to change
So little effort to do the right thing
Clinging to the arrogance
That is the human way of life
Hearts filled with nothing more
Than selfish whims to be coddled
From sunrise to sunset
Turning the sun bright red in the smoke

And yet the fire burns on
Until nature rises up
To rain down and correct the course
Leaving humans scurrying from the storm
To find the higher ground they destroyed
Greed can't save us from our apathy
Look at the fire licking the sky
As callous hearts and broken hearts
Suffer the same

The Earth will have her way

Snow Devours

Mountains of snow
Devour summer's vegetation
Blanketing green in white
Freezing all life beneath
Suspending all growth
Awaiting the thaw
To discover
What survives
The hungry snow
Devouring all in its wake
Leaving us with hope
The thaw will nourish the ground
It hides
Creating hills around plants
And berms on porches
While trapping inside
Those ill-equipped to explore
The frozen whiteness
Covering all signs of life
In a snowy grave

Truth and Denial

Sshhh!
Don't speak
Forget the truth
It lives in the shadows
Afraid of the light
Wishing to be what
It can never be
When the lie
Screams louder
Than the truth
We begin to believe
In a life that never existed
That never can exist
But if we just keep quiet
Don't speak a single word
We can keep convincing ourselves
The lies we tell are the truth
And the truth hiding in the shadows
Are the lies
And then we build a world built on lies
A world hurtling toward extinction
Because the truth is far too difficult
The truth demands we accept responsibility
The truth demands we be accountable
The truth demands we take action
It's so much easier
To imprison truth in rhetoric
Than to release it
And accept the consequences
The problem is our denial
No matter how sweet

Will turn sour
Because a lie will fade away
But the truth
The truth we refuse to face
The truth will continue to exist
No matter how much we deny it
And, then, the consequences
Will be all the more deadly...

Silence Must End

Silence is no longer an option
When your words destroy
The world we know
I must speak mine in an effort
To repair the damage you've done
I won't stand idly by while you destroy
The air we breathe
The water we drink
The ground where we grow food
The forests that give us oxygen
The bees who pollinate our fruit
The freedoms we enjoy
To speak our minds
To worship or not
To assemble
To investigate those in power
No, I will not go silent
While you trample on
Everyone and everything
I hold in my heart
The very life I live
You don't get to destroy me
Just because your beliefs
Cast me as the enemy
In the script you write
To justify
The suffering you inflict
With your words
That lead to destruction
In an arc away from compassion
In a world that destroys justice

In a circle that explodes the truth
All in the name of greed
My silence must end now

Recycled Breath

The wind blows between here and there
I wonder if it takes my tears with it
Does the world realize
What we breathe out someone else breathes in
You might be recycling my breath right now
Or I might be recycling yours
A connection across oceans and mountains
Resting in each of us for a moment before travelling on
To the next and the next and the next
I feel the wind on my back and wonder if it's your breath
Propelling me forward even though you long to pull me back
As I move into that place you can't come
Where my experience diverges from yours
And we seek to understand how to find connection
In our differences
A quiet wind blows between you and me
A storm wind picks up momentum as we
Lose sight of the breath that binds us
Recycled time and again
So that we all breathe each other
In a sigh that refuses to deny
What we see when we look into the eye
Of a lover lost or a newborn child
And let out that deep breath
We'd been holding so as to hold on
To everything we were or can be
So I ask you
Do you know where the breath you take originated?
Perhaps it exhaled from your favorite person on Earth
Or your worst enemy
But, you say, it's been cleansed by the trees

And it's trip from here to there or there to here
The air we breathe
Traversing around the world
Carrying with it a small part of each of us
Why would we pollute that air with hatred?
Why would we fill that air with toxins?
Why would we deny that breath we need?
So I ask you one last time
To join me in a large inhale and exhale of love

When the End Comes

When the end comes
Leaving us with no more beginnings
Will we finally see what we had in common
Will we finally see how our differences complemented
Will we finally see our humanity
In that final moment when all is over
Where will we stand
As we fall over the cliff
Into an abyss
While the Earth takes over
Destroying those who sought to exploit
With the destructive greed
Fight as we might
Until the bitter end
The consequences will kill us all
When the end finally comes

Stark Sky

Stark, bare branches sway
Against a dark, cloudy sky
Devoid of love's touch

Message on a Hummingbird's Wing

A hummingbird hovered in the air
Wings fluttering in a blur
Almost invisible in between the tree's leaves
It looked like it had a message to impart
I watched it fluttering, hovering, whirring
Just out of reach
Teasing and taunting my cat
Mesmerizing me with its movement
A moment later it disappeared in a
Green and yellow blur against a bright blue sky
And I wondered if the peace I felt
Emanated from that small encounter
Then my cat tugged her leash
And brought me back to reality
Whatever the hummingbird tried to communicate
Was only a matter of my interpretation
My perspective felt a ping of introspection
At the mere presence of the hovering hummingbird
And then it was gone
Evaporated with the hummingbird's departure

Revolves and Rotates

You and I
Walking along
Never paying attention
To the ground beneath
The sky above
The air around
Until the ground shakes
The sky breaks
The air suffocates
Then we ask
What can we count on

The Earth revolves and rotates

You and I
Going about our day
Driven by expectations
To buy
To possess
To accumulate
Never paying attention
Until
The house shakes
The possessions break
The clutter suffocates
Then we ask
What can we count on

The Earth revolves and rotates

You and I

Lost in our drama
Unwilling to lend a helping hand
To those we don't understand
To those who have less than
To those who are different than
Never paying attention
Until
Our hearts break
Our bank account shakes
Our isolation suffocates
Then we ask
What can we count on

The Earth revolves and rotates

But what if that stops, too....

The Earth Sighs

The Earth sighs
She watches as they fill the air with poison
She tastes the plastic they dump in the streams
She listens to the crashing of trash being piled on her ground
She feels the ash of burning forests
She watches as the humans destroy their own habitat
People destroying her resources
Taking what they want for artificial greed
Thinking they have power over.... Her
But
But
But
She laughs as their greed kills them
Because she knows that someday
After they're gone
She'll heal her air, her streams, her soil
And maybe the next evolution of Earthlings
Will finally get it right
The Earth sighs

Ardor Exits

Rooted in ardor
Traveling toward the sky
Leaves exit branches

Worst Case Earth

Your hand ripped from mine
Walking along
Silence, foreboding and cruel
Dividing us
As we move forward apart
Into new challenges
Hills and streams
Mountains and valleys
Oceans and deserts
Breaking what's before us
Reminiscent of what once was
Separately seeing what's broken
Because of greed and hate
Trees dying
Streams cloudy with pollution
Food filled with poison
Air that fills lungs with death
Destroying what took millions of years to create
Will your money save you now?
As the Earth crumbles into dust
Nothing left for the next generation to fix
Humanity's future coming to an end
The Earth ready to reclaim her future
The Earth ready to reclaim herself

Call Me When the World Ends

We ride this merry-go-round
Round and round and round
Looking out at the decay
Seeing the beauty in destruction
Feeling numb to the view
Today, tomorrow, yesterday
News of the same old things
Exchange one day for the next
Without even noticing
Except for the date at the bottom of the screen
Life goes forward and backward
Stomping on progress
Pulling the tethers that keep us in place
So we keep at it
Day after day after day
Greed destroying the very thing it needs to survive
The Earth implodes
While we sleepwalk through our days
And fantasize through our nights
Pretending like nothing we do can change the outcome
So I'll just stare at the waves until they crash on my head
And, maybe, just maybe you'll
Call me when the world ends

What's Left?

What's left?
When you take the money
When you take the wealth
When we stand in the ruins
All the symbols of austerity
Scattered to the ends of time
Clock ticking down to the closing bell
The market no longer ticking along
Power over Earth's inhabitants lost
Money no longer ruling you and me
When our bondage to the dollar is broken
When we are no longer slaves to our bank accounts
When we break the chains of material possessions
Do we fight each other for the meager leftovers
Do we learn to work together to forge a new beginning
Wealth no longer dividing us into the classes we deny
Do we finally admit our dream has turned to nightmare
Do we see that the bits and bytes representing worthless paper
Are lost to us forever in a crashed world
Left with nothing to represent wealth
Is destruction of all we cherish
Where we finally find
The wealth we idolize
Leaves us bereft
When the gold melts
When the paper burns
When coal becomes more valuable than diamonds
What's left?
Love… compassion…peace…

Dry Riverbed

Upon a dry riverbed
I found a bouquet of rocks
Bright and smooth
Veins of reds, grays, blacks, and whites
Specked with sparkles
Arranged as if by a talented hand
Drawing me ever closer
Stepping over craggy rocks
Traversing dry, arid earth
I struggled to reach those rocks
Thinking them a treasure in the midst of ruin
A sign that all wasn't destroyed by drought
Inflicted when the rain dried up
I desperately needed to believe there was hope
In the middle of the dry riverbed
Left behind when the rain stopped
And the sun blazed without relent
Stripping the land of moisture and life
I stared at the bouquet of rocks calling my name
Saw love pulse from them like the ground's heart
Seeking nourishment
I reached the bouquet
Feet covered in cuts and bruises
Dust burning each one
Legs aching from the effort
I fell on the bouquet of rocks
Tears fell from my eyes
The beauty overwhelmed me
Rain began to gently fall once again
Splashing upon the rocks
Pooling on the cracked, arid grounds

Soaking into the earth
Feeding its thirst
I turned my crying eyes toward the sky
As the rain slid over my skin
The water covered the rocks upon which I stood
They shimmered and glowed under the pooling rain
Tempting me to stay even as
The water rushed by me turning the dry riverbed
Into a river once again

Dear Billionaires

Waking up in a world
Where your money
No longer holds worth
What will you be then?
When all you cherish
Means nothing
Nothing elevates you
Above those you
Step on to hoard your wealth
What will you do then?
When your ability to eat
Depends on those you derided
Because they got in your way
On your path to filling the void
In your psyche
What will you value then?
Do you ever think about the damage
You inflict on the world, the earth, the people
In your drive for profits to fill your full pockets?
What will you do when all you value means nothing?
What will you do when the Earth you've destroyed
Levels the playing field and you discover
You're not so different than those you malign?
I just wonder do you ever think about this kind of future?

Dirt

Plowed earth
Showing your underbelly
Deep, dark, rich soil
Filled with all the nutrients
Essential for nourishing all life
The rich smell
Filling the air
Reminding us all
You own us
As much as we try to believe
We own you

Water

I sip you
I gulp you
I savor you
Clear, cool, smooth
More soothing than the finest wine
More refreshing than the sweetest juice
More invigorating than the largest coffee
Offering me a future
Sparkling or still
Enhancing my life
With every drop consumed
Warm or icy cold
Offering just what my body needs
Perfection quenching my thirst

In Flight

Alight in flight
Soaring above human drama
The bird sees it all
The destruction of progress
The destitution of greed
As humans go about their business
Striving for power
Never realizing
The bird possesses the greatest power of all
The power to soar without the pull of possessions
Flying through the sky with feathers and family
Friends join the party
Soaring above the Earth
Flying to warmth when cold weather hits
Flying north when temperatures rise too high
Home being where the bird lands
Perhaps the bird even feels at home while in flight
Sometimes I wonder if the bird laments human existence
In all its pettiness and greed
Today I strive to remember the bird and I
Inhabit the same Earth
As I fly through the air returning to my home
On a huge metal machine
Allowing me take flight
Much like the bird

Resilient Fern

The fern
Blows in the wind
Dappled by sunshine
Branches casting shadows across it
Rooting itself in the moment
Lacy leaves tipped brown
Thirsty for a rainfall
Seeking to spread
Even as it dies back
Not quite dead
Only dormant
Pulling in nutrients
From the decay around it
To come back stronger than ever
Never losing sight of its purpose
Holding itself strong without seeing
The beauty it offers all who see it
A flash of green in a sea of brown
Never losing itself to the forest around it
But always standing its ground
Even when uprooted and moved
Against its will to a new home
Far from all it knows
Finding a way to thrive in
A city far from its forest home

Drowning

Therein lies the loss
Temptation floating by
Desire frozen in a glacier
Melting in the sun's gaze
Breaking away from its foundation
Moving toward you and me
Destruction inevitable
As I face what I once felt so sure about
As doubt rises over me like a wave
In a turbulent sea
Seeking to exact revenge
On shorelines polluting the edges of life
Where nothing remains intact
Deception poisoning everything that's left
Water rushing by in torrents of rising sea levels
As the ground fractures and shifts
Earthquakes realigning the ocean floor
To remake the borders we claim
Shrinking our arrogance to humility
Because underneath these clouds
Roars the wind that changes everything
Lifts us up and slams us down
Time and again
Trying to get our attention
As we go about our lives
Ruled by a world that only exists
Within the constructs of conformity
Unwilling to defy beliefs even in the face of facts
The truth should set us free
But it can only do that if we're willing to see it
Will our last gasp of air before we drown

In a world flooded with toxicity
Be the acknowledgment that denial didn't serve us
Or will it be an insistence that clinging to belief will save us

Uprooted Existence

I stood before you
Uprooted
My underside exposed
My lifeline reaching for nourishment
Finding air where soil should be
Suffocating on the wrong nourishment
Filled with the loss of something I couldn't change
Soil drying and falling away in the bright sunshine
To parts better accustomed to the dark
The dark, dark nourishment
Ready to give me strength
And hold me in place
Until that moment
I pulled away from my foundation
Fell on my side
My leaves and limbs
Crashing toward the soil
Away from the sun they needed
As everything in my existence changed
Upside down
My top finding the soil
My roots loved so much
As I struggled to find everything
To give me the nourishment I so craved
As my world turned upside down
Leaving me completely
Uprooted
Seeking a way to survive
With roots facing the sun
And my top facing the soil
Everything lost its place

Disorienting me
As the Earth continued its journey
With little regard for my upside-down existence
And I wondered just how long I could survive
My uprooted existence

Silver Lining

Every cloud has a silver lining
At least that's what people say
I've often wondered
If I fell through a cloud
Would the silver come with me
Would it replenish itself
Or if perchance I happened
To lie upon a cloud
I might just discover that
Every cloud has a filthy lining
Soiling my dreams
With ruined possibility
Because twisted inside
Every silver lining exists a cloud
Imagine the maze
Cloud
Silver lining
Cloud
Silver lining
And on it goes
Until
The core discloses
A gold lining under a cloud
As we ignore how the life we live
Is nothing more than a
Cycle against suicide
That slowly kills us as we deceive ourselves
That silver linings make clouds bright
Rather than face the fact our actions
Destroy all that keeps us alive while
Sulfur dioxide creates bright clouds

And poisons us into a world of deception
That we can do whatever we want
To our world because hope survives
Regardless of our destructive behavior
Regardless of our disregard for humanity
Regardless of our indifference toward life
We comfort ourselves with the idea
That absolute truth came from the lips of the one
Who said every cloud has a silver lining

My Magnolia

The bloom opened
Magnificent
Snowy white
Larger than my hand
Surrounded by
Dark green rubbery leaves
On a tree reaching toward
The clouds floating above
In a blue sky
Not a drop of rain in sight
On that warm summer day
The first bloom
On the tree
You gifted me
Simply because you saw
The joy in my eyes
As I imagined the blooms
The magnolia would provide
How I wish
That beautiful tree
Would never outgrow our yard
But, alas, I know the day will come
Just as it seems
Everything outgrows its home
Ready to either move on
Or find unwarranted destruction
Did I act with selfishness
When I longed for that beautiful
Evergreen magnolia
To show me its blooms
Year after year after year

In a yard too small
For its lifetime
I shortened its life
Just to give myself joy
I convince myself
Every time I look at it
That its life will be long and floral
Because its growth will outlast us all
Yet, there's that little twinge of guilt
Each time I smile at its
Magnificent blooms

Part of the Machine

We are all part of
The machine
Creating and destroying
In equal measure
Doing our part to
Prop up systems
We don't believe in
But can't escape
Living, loving, losing
The Earth we call home
Thinking ourselves
Better than we are
But just look at how it all works
We, even the rebels, play their part
To keep the system intact
Even those harmed by the system
Keep buying into its worst aspects
Playing on our fears and rage
To keep us running on a wheel
That gives us no way to get off
No matter what we say we want
Defaulting back to what was
Over and over
Stepping forward
Stepping backward
Stepping sideways
This dance keeps us working
In the machine
We claim we want to destroy
As we watch the Earth around us
Move ever closer to expelling us

In order to start rebuilding its machine
With beings more in tuned to playing
Creative roles instead of destructive ones
Accept your place in the machine
What else can you possibly do?

Life Goes On

Waves on the river
Snaking toward the sea
Crashing into boulders
Breaking leaves to crumbs
Tumbling dropped branches
Taking with it all the memories
Haunting the forest
Dreaming of a future
Standing tall for centuries
Outliving species after species
Growing from the leftovers
Recycling every tiny morsel
Morphing into new life

Empty Message

I wrote you a message
Hoping you'd read between the lines
Of words that said so little
And spaces that said so much
I rolled up the message
Slid it into a blue balloon
Blew air into the balloon
Until it was as round as a ball
Tied off the end
Encapsulating my message
Of the unsaid to you
Set it adrift on a windy day
Apologized to the Earth for the pollution
Watched my message
Float across the air
In your direction
Growing smaller with each inch it moved
Turned my back as I lost sight of it
Heard a distant crack of thunder
Knew that like so many other times
The message I sent you would go
Unheard, unspoken, undelivered
If I had the courage to fill in the spaces
Between the nothing I said
With the something in my heart
Maybe I'd be brave enough
To guarantee delivery
Instead of destruction
Instead I ask you to
Read what I refuse to say
Understand what I refuse to explain

Respond to what I refuse to deliver
With all these messages in the empty spaces

Previously appeared on Write with TLC and Medium

Poppies Dance

Poppies still grow amidst the dead weeds
In the abandoned flowerbeds
On the estate where life once flourished
Their bright orange blooms mocking
The untended landscape
Where intentions grew unfertilized
Until they depleted the soil
Leaving only the dreams behind
To wither in the sun
To freeze in the snow
To blow away on the wind
Searching for more fertile ground
To take root and grow to the moon
The poppies held their ground
Waiting to feed off the decomposing plants
Rotting their nutrients back into the soil
Dying to nourish the dreams left behind
The poppies dance in glorious rhythm

Previously appeared on YouTube

Beach Breaks

Seek the beach
Where the sea
Weathers the sand
Draped with shells
See all the traps
Set at all angles
Grab the stars
Stare at the sparkle
Seals beware
Trash appears as gems
Battered and beaten
Ever the least ready
After the cast has left
Even as the day sets
Weave me a new basketcase
Crazy panes of glass
Break my wave
Leave me a grave
As a tender hand
Reaches beneath my heart
Wraps heat as an eternal cape
The effect leaves me agape
The beach breaks my heart

Hanging Words

The words hang between us
Hints and double-talk
Leaving us on tiptoe
Touching the truth
With a forked tongue
Poisoning every little thought
With doubt
While the words that matter
Hide in the folds of experience
Watching the truth die
In an avalanche of unyielding attack
On all that's good and right and real
Just to keep the power players playing
So we listen for the words that matter
As we pray to a god who long ago deafened to us
Because the only god that matters is power
The power to control
The power to hold
The power to own
The power to destroy
All for the sake of pumping up egos
That can't figure out how to survive
In the destruction they wreak
To the home where they live
To the home where we all live
Because the intoxication of power
Keeps them addicted to their master
And so the story goes
Words that obfuscate
Words that titillate
Words that divide

Oh, the power of words
To wield the weapon of divisiveness
Hanging between the people
Who most need to unite

Nectar is for the Birds

Nectar is for the birds
Hummingbirds, orioles
Drink to their fill
The others flitter by
Uninterested
Intent on seeds and nuts
A little fruit to whet the appetite
Leaving lots of nectar for the bees
To spread from bloom to bloom
Bringing fruit to bear
Sometimes we just must see
What's for the birds
Isn't so bad as it seems

Outrunning the Toxicity of Secrets

Hoof beats across the desert plain
Uprooting the secrets hiding in the hard ground
Pounding them into dust
Swirling around the beautiful manes and tails
Blinding the horses
As they try to outrun your secret
Settling into their coats
Their eyes frantic with fear
As they try to outrun
This secret destroying their home
At the end of the desert plain
They stopped and looked back
One last whinny with forelegs raised pawing the air
The horses turn, drop their feet, shake off your secret
And run...
Run...
Run...
Into the depths of the forest
Hiding from the destruction your secret
Wrought upon their world
Driving them out of their homes
Like so many before them

Secrets turn to dust
When exposed to the sun
But even their dust is toxic

Veil of Clouds

Hidden behind a veil of clouds
The moon peeks out
Teasing the world with light
Haloing above the clouds
Like a crown anointing royalty
Too shy to step forward and claim
Her rightful place in the sky
Bowing to the light of the sun
Ruling the night with great reflection
Lighting the way for the night traveler
Looking for a treasure of love and affection
Or perhaps just shared lust
The moon flirts with the clouds and the stars
And the travelers beneath
Offering itself as both servant and ruler
Reflecting the glory of day into night
While the stars twinkle around it
Winking their own secret hiding
Behind a veil of clouds

East of Never

Turn right on the highway
Head right into the mountains
Stop in the valley to smell the flowers
Take a left turn at the creek
Keep moving around the mountain
Circling the mountain until you reach the peak
Looking east, west, north and south
Seeing everything you destroyed on your journey
Eroded soil and broken boulders
Uprooted trees and stomped wildflower blooms
Listen for the birds you can't hear
Look for the butterflies you can't see
Sniff the air for fir trees you can't smell
Touch the barren ground you can't feel
Taste the poisoned water you can't taste
Then head east of never
Where your money and power mean nothing
Where no one will be waiting for you
Where you will have to recognize
You can't fix what you destroyed
On your quest to conquer the world

Life Cycle

The tulips open wide
Revealing their inner beauty
Like legs and arms spread
In a downpour of sunshine
Feeling the kiss of the bee
Feeding on its nectar
Waiting for the moment of its release
A single petal drops on a wet rock
Red and yellow against the cinnamon
The wind lifts the petal
It waves through the air
Leaving behind all its siblings
Knowing it can't return
It's broken from the family
The single petal doesn't know
All the others will soon drop as well
Taking their own journeys across the wind
Landing in some unknown place
Never knowing where the bee took the nectar
Withering, drying, over-saturated
Returning to the soil to feed another
Unwitting in its life cycle
But essential to the cycle of life
But for a moment its beauty sparkled in the
Sunlit and dewy morning

Waiting on Tomorrow

Smoke fills the air
Between truth and deception
A fire smoldering with fear
A spark leaping over the barrier
To burn the dry leaves
And scorch the earth where we sit
We watch with detached indifference
Thinking someone should do something
Yet, we sip champagne in cracked crystal glasses
As we toast what once was
As the smoke rises toward the sky
Blocking our view of the moon and the stars
Even the clouds can't be found
As we look for someone, somewhere
To fix what we spent decades, centuries, breaking
Because we wanted what we wanted when we wanted it
So we set the world on fire and watched it burn
For the pleasure of seeing the flames dance
Without ever once pausing to ask the most important
question
The answer so obvious
That's tomorrow's problem
Until the day tomorrow finally comes
Leaving us with no more tomorrows…

Nature Renewal

The nature of man
To destroy what he consumes
Seeks Earth's renewal

Sea Creatures

Waves crash against the rocks
The depths beneath quiet
Wind and sun and rain
Unseen in the deep dark water
Seaweed dancing
Undiscovered life darting in between the strands
All unaware of the damage wrought above
Going about living as they always have
Interwoven into nature
Playing their role
Roles those above might not ever know
But that might be vital to survival
As the pollution from above sinks down
Confusing all the creatures only trying to survive
Playing their roles in the life of the Earth
Being killed by the greed and advancement of those above
Who can't seem to understand they're killing themselves
As they kill the sea creatures below by disrupting the planet
They need to survive
Makes one wonder who really is the more advanced species

Ignite the World

A single flame
Bursting into an inferno
A dry leaf blowing across
The deserted life
We left behind
A building holding the memories
We held in the cages of yesterday
To hold us up above the present
As we reached for the future
Floating away on that flame
Landing on everything we held dear
Wondering if we can remember
That moment we captured on film
Because we wanted to hold on to it forever
The flames reaching into the sky
Reminding us the future is never guaranteed
As our tears slip across the terrain under our feet
Trying to escape the world burning around us
That we stripped of every opportunity to recover
In our zeal to add to our coffers at every turn
Nothing left here to see as the world we created
Burns to ashes and taunts us with our own greed

Nature Rules

There is no immortality
We will all die
It's the nature of life
To work toward death
So we live the best we can
Trying to create a legacy
So our lives will mean something
To someone somewhere
That's the way it works
We fight until the bitter end
Trying to subdue nature
Even as it proves time and again
Nature rules
Long after we've lost our lives
Nature will recreate what we destroy
And it will use us to do so

Night of Truth

We counted the clouds above our heads
One less than the night before
But who could possibly know for sure
Maybe we miscounted
Maybe one hid tonight
Maybe one floated away
As clouds are wont to do
We needed the rain that teased
But those clouds weren't that kind of cloud
You reached for me
We couldn't stand this much longer
The moment of truth lay in this night
As we looked over the drought-laden land
Without rain you and I would soon wither and die
Nothing left to be remembered by
Not even a seed to drop into the dusty ground
To carry forth the cycle of life
At least we'd go out together
Just as we'd started

Iris

Will I ever see the
Faqqua iris?
Will it open its beauty
For my eyes to see?
Defying the destruction
Wrought on its habitat
By those who hold no value
In the land they destroy
People and fauna destroyed
In equal measure in the name of greed
Excusing the destruction by belief
In a god they claim created
All they destroy
How can that be?
Nature will find a way and who knows
The Faqqua iris just might survive
Longer than any human alive

Gravel Road

Tires crunch across me
Moving far too fast
Or far too slow
The faster the drive
The more dust I throw up
Communicating your speed
Is dangerous for you
The dip coming up
Will throw you off
The car moving too fast
Proves its inhabitants
As unsure as the car
Moving too slow
Both are playing a game
Trying to figure out
Exactly why I'm so rough
No one ever told them
I'm older than they'll ever be
A beer can tossed from the window
Joins many others along with
Soda cans and candy wrappers
People forget that they are the ones
Who destroy the pristine nature they seek
As they seek to escape their concrete lives
In search of the nature all around me

Outpace Life

The pace at which you move
Makes molasses look like water
This holding pattern we've been trapped in
As we try to outpace reality
Must give way someday
We can't keep pretending life lasts forever
I watch the minute hand move like a secondhand
As the space between us outpaces our efforts
To the change the circumstances
That lead us to this place where we promise
To pick up pace next time around
But will there be a next time
Or is this our only time?
Lost in the pace of the world
Losing its grip on itself
As we destroy all that's before us
To race past to some desired outcome
As if we can outrun death
In pursuit of all the things
That death takes anyway

Between the Past and the Future

You slid into the empty space
Between the past and the future
Ignoring the pain that came before
Pretending what lay ahead was secure
I stood in the present and watched you
Take up space you didn't earn
In a world you worked to dismantle
While pretending you were constructing it
Your greed destroyed the space
Between the past and the future
Your hate uprooted the connections
Between the past and the future
Your cruelty violated the hope
Between the past and the future
I wonder
What I could've done
What I should've done
What I wish I would've done
When you slid into that empty space
Between the past and the future
With your never-ending need for power...

The Owl's Warning

The owl hoots
From its perch
High in the spruce tree
A forest burning around it
Sending out a warning to those below
Run for your lives
Our home is under attack
Burning to the ground
Taking flight to high perch after high perch
Sounding the same alarm
To friends and enemies alike
There are no allies or foes
When your world is burning to the ground
Sound the alarm before you take flight
Flee together for safe ground
When there's nothing left to save of your home
Until one day there's nowhere left to move
Because the only thing left is the ashes
As the owl flies overheard
Crying out a warning
No one can heed
That turns to a cry of grief
For all that's been lost

Broken Earth

We broke the Earth
In our effort to bend
Her to our will
Stripping her resources
Polluting her water
Poisoning her air
Contaminating her soil
All in the name of progress
And greed
And power
Convincing ourselves
Of her indestructibility
As we took what we wanted
Without regard for consequences
But our broken Earth will have the last laugh
She'll put herself back together
Even if she kills us in the process
So really all we've done is
Break ourselves

Last Hope

The territory we walked
Without the caution we needed
Because we just couldn't guess
What the delicate jar held inside
You insisted I carry it with both hands
Because there might be a prize inside
Or a key to a future
Where blue skies would offer cover
And fluffy white clouds would linger
But the question we couldn't bear to ask
Would the release be worth the wait
As we walked in the shade of the dwindling forest
Counting on a fortune awaiting us
If we could find our way through the present
But what we most wanted was to skip ahead
To the part where no one played the fool
And we could share a moment of revelation
Instead of standing in the margin
Our nimble step moving us forward
As we set a match to the mistakes of yesterday
And prayed our salvation was somewhere in space
Holding on to a picture of the perfect utopia
Where we could wander with abandon
And not worry about a tangle of webs
Sucking the oxygen from our hopes and dreams
Maybe we could dazzle the world with the jar
We placed in a frayed and abandoned satchel
And hid underneath a broken chair
Hoping we could save it from the anchor
Determined to dash it to pieces

Expand Your Territory

Add a dash of love
To anchor us in this moment
Don't just sit in the chair
Hiding your satchel full of hope
That could dazzle our future
With oxygen to give life to the present
As we tangle with each other over the truth
Pushing us to wander in different directions
As we can't agree on the picture of the Earth we want
Traveling through space on a trajectory we can't control
As I try to match your hate-filled rhetoric with love-filled words
The truth never feels quite as nimble as your lies
As you push those who don't look like you to the margin
Refusing to even share space with them
I'd call you a fool, but somehow I think you'd like it
As you skip along the path of your willful ignorance
Refusing the truth of the present moment as if it's poison
All because you'd rather cling to your fortune than offer solutions
To the missing shade we all need to find from the blazing hate
Release yourself from the prison of conventional beliefs
Question the authority telling you to hate the other person
Linger here in this moment of love and kindness
Maybe we can turn the dark skies blue
If we understand the key is to address the greed
But if the only prize you can see is power over people
You'll carry us all into a dark, limited, and lifeless future
Where a jar of water will be more valuable than gold
But I guess your mind is made up
Every caution I've tried to express is lost on you
As you expand your territory to expand your power

Quiet Yesterdays

Yesterday I was quiet
I listened to every beat
As the words bounced
Off the alley walls
And got lost in the traffic
Speeding by
All the words broke
The world we knew into tiny pieces
I watched as bricks disintegrated beneath
Hatred spewed with venom
Snaking its way into the heart and minds
Of so many people just trying to survive
Trapped in a cocoon where truth was the lie
And the lie was the truth
Never knowing what to believe
One ends up believing nothing
As the world crumbles
The loss of what once was
A mere shadow of what could be
In an alley where we hide
Just to fight another day
And wonder if the quiet yesterdays
Cost us more than we knew

Not Today

The Earth crumbles
At our feet
As we walk miles
To find our way
Wishing for a place
Where peace could reign
And love could rule
Watching the destruction
All around us
As the sky darkens
And the air turns ashy
Our bodies scorching
Under the sun
Where once there was shade
Trees blackened to charcoal
Reminding us of backyard barbecues
We trek on slowly gaining ground
Across a world where greed and ideology
Destroyed everything in its path
I look toward you and wonder
If we can survive this
If we even want to survive this
Somewhere on the other side of all this
We're convinced we'll find others
Willing to unite for our cause
Of creating peace and harmony
Of spreading love and truth
Of healing the hurt
Of repairing the broken
As our feet grow tired
And our bodies grow weary

We look for a place to rest
And realize today won't be the day
We find what we're looking for
But tomorrow we'll try again
No matter how many times
Today isn't the day
Because that's who we are

When the Blue Fades

Blue fades to gray
In a sky losing its light
As the clouds gather
In a world hellbent
On profiting on paradise
There's nothing left
As smoke fills the air
From the destruction
Wrought by humans
In search of filling voids
With the latest status symbol
Unwilling to sacrifice the material
For the greater good
Unable to see the bigger picture
Beyond their own greed
Unprepared for a future
They can't imagine will differ from today
As the rainbow fades away
Leaving us with only black and white
The voids of color filling lives lost
Begging us to find a way to reverse
The destruction
Willing a future where
Gray fades to blue

Wild Release into the Tame

Have you ever seen the look
In the eyes of a deer
Trying to find its way back
To the wild
Seeking the forest beyond
The suburban streets
That overtook its home
Destroying its food supply
Asphalting its forest floor
Cutting down its shade trees
All for the sake of more homes
Little cookie cutter homes
That cut up the forest and the fields
Leaving behind little trace
In the non-native plants
Replacing the familiar plants
The deer knows as home
How many forests must we tame
Pushing all its inhabitants into
Cities and suburbs where they can't survive
Then we wonder why all these wild animals
Wander our streets where they're not wanted
Where, oh, where are they supposed to go
When we've released the tame into their wild
And their wild into our tame

Healing Hubris

Worm crawls in sick soil
Hidden from crass overlords
Healing our hubris

Personal Gain

The Earth rotated again today
The Earth revolved a bit more today
Humans destroyed a bit more today
Excusing their destruction as just
Part of the way things are
Somehow seeing their nature as destructive
Gives them license to avoid change
Listen to how I speak
Separating myself from other humans
As if I am any better with the excuses I make
For the destruction I create as I journey
Through life one more day and then one more
Because this small destruction can't possibly matter
But when my small destruction is added
To all the other small destructions
The end result is a world that becomes
Increasingly less inhabitable for humans
And not just humans
But innocent beings just going about their business
One day at a time
Oblivious to the danger they face
Day after day from the hubris of humans
Destroying the Earth they inhabit
All for their own personal gain

Symbiosis

Green grass fading to yellow
Yellow grass drying to brown
As the leaves fall from the evergreen tree
Carpeting the ground
Hiding the roots searching for water
Soil hardens until it strangles
All that tries to grow in it
The soil that can't quite nourish
The tree that doesn't belong here
Because we want the moment of nostalgia
Instead of honoring the present
Creating a yard filled with plants
That would thrive somewhere else
While they struggle to survive here
All because we don't want to accept reality
So we destroy the plant, the soil, the water
All to force what doesn't belong
In spite of the destruction we wreak
Because we want what we want
No matter the greater cost
Then we question why
The plant that doesn't belong
Just can't live
And the world around it suffers
Because if we just planted what belonged
It would be nourished and return the favor

Beginning Our Extinction

The beginning never seemed real
It just happened as we took that step
The one that we thought didn't matter
Do we even remember when this began?
I keep looking back for the beginning
But every beginning I find pushes me farther back
To another beginning of this history we condemn
When did it really begin?
Do we have to find the beginning of this history
To figure out how to change the future
How to fix our mistakes
How to write an ending we can live with
Or are we stuck with this beginning
Driving us to extinction

Resolution Resolves Nothing

The resolution sounded good
It laid out all the flowers
Ignored the thorns
Trimmed the weeds
Fertilized the soil
Yet, it changed nothing
You explained it like a Spring bloom
Blossoming into a flower
Flowering into fruit
I nodded loving
The sound of an orchard
Of wildflowers and fruit trees
A virtual garden paradise
But then I reached for a flower
Felt the thorns and briers
Attach to my skin
Smelled the dung
Saw the blooms dropping
The flowers wilting
The fruit rotting
Understood finally
You never meant to resolve anything
Only to paint a veneer over
The truth so no one could see
The destruction you wrought
In the name of greed
When a resolution could have been
So easy
So invigorating
So fruitful
For all parties involved

You took the opportunity
To create a resolution
That left us all with nothing

The World in Peril

The world in peril
By its very nature
Creating a hierarchy
Of inhabitants
That rob resources
To feed greed
And leave behind
Nothing worth keeping
In their search for immortality
Choosing to destroy their own home
With the arrogance
That they'll just find another one
To destroy all over again
Because what's another world
In peril
When one can fill one's pockets
With riches that won't matter much
Once the world in peril perishes

Finally Piqued

The peak of the mountain
Peeked over the rooftop
Covered in snow
As the sun shined bright above
To the east
And dark clouds rolled in
From the west
Piquing my curiosity
About how we handle
The chaos of the ever changing
World in which we live
The cold day that should be warm
And the hot day that should be cold
Taking us on a trip we never understood
As we watch the snowy summit melt
And wonder whether we'll survive
The changes we brought on ourselves
As we deny our responsibility
And refuse all accountability
Until that day when it's too late
And then we cry and scream and kick
Why didn't someone tell me?
Only to hear a resounding
Why didn't you listen?
And we know it's too late
To save ourselves
As we peek back at all we ignored
Our interest finally piqued

How Are We Supposed To Survive This?

How are we supposed to survive this?
You asked with tears in your eyes
I shrugged
How the hell was I supposed to know?
It was all new to me, too.
Never in my wildest imagination did I see this
We stood on the bridge we'd built together
Stared at the stream below
Jagged rocks and quagmires stared back at me
Where once love had run freely gifting us with life
All that was left was the remnants of the explosion
Intended to bring us closer as it destroyed all that had been
So we could discover peace through violence
The jagged rocks shook their head at our ignorance
The quagmires laughed at our self-deception
I turned to look at you
When had violence become the only answer anyone considered?
This wasn't the world I wanted to live in
The love emanating from my heart spilled onto the dry creek bed
Shined against the rock for a second before being absorbed
Somewhere on this journey love got left behind
Creating drought and war and famine in a world crying out for
More, more, more
So we fed it hate and possessions and money and fear
Until it gorged itself and exploded
Taking everything good with it
I felt a tear trail down my cheek
Staring at a world that appeared desolate and destroyed
Where did all our greed take us?
The greed we thought would give us power
What good is power when there's nothing left

So I ask you the question you asked me
How the hell do we survive this?

Suicidal Ones

Under the bridge
With the water rushing by
We stood in quiet surrender
To the tumultuous life
We tried to leave behind
The past that haunts us
The deception we wove
Into a quilt that chilled us
Fraying with every truth
That dared to thread a needle
We watched that water
And prayed to the water gods
To take away all the pain
We didn't want to face
As we watched the swirling water
Rise
Rise
Rise
Raindrops falling
Snow melting
Mud flowing
Drowning the rocks
Washing leaves downstream
Fish struggling to swim
All we could see disappearing
In that cold, cold night
Where the stars refused to shine
Where the clouds blanketed the moon
And our quilt grew ever thinner
Because the truth will
Eventually

Burst the seams of deception
Leaving everything uncovered and raw
Tears froze on our faces
As we watched
Everything our ancestors fought for
Disappear in a cloud of greedy smoke
Consuming the very land where we stood
We jumped from rock to rock
Screaming until our breath evaporated
About the injustice of the corruption
Stealing our very lives
Until the water rose
Above our heads
Above the bridge
Above the dark of night
We swam hard
Reached for the moon
Pleaded with the Earth
Who took back the life
She'd gifted us with
Reminding us
We're the fragile ones
We're the destructive ones
We're the suicidal ones
Humans can't seem to understand
What we do here
Affects what happens there
But, oh,
The Earth
The Earth
The Earth
She'll outlive us all

Not on My Watch

The water rises above
All our heads in a tumultuous sea
Of broken souls and bruised hearts
Driving us to see
You and I aren't so different
When all we're doing is gasping for air
As the tide pulls us under time and again
Crashing us into the sea
Where the water refuses to let us swim
So we reach out for a hand, any hand
To lift us from the depths
Of the hate drowning love
And swear
Not on my watch
Not on my watch
Will you destroy the world I know
Even as the waves toss us to and fro
Filling our mouths with sand
Banging our heads against cliffs
As we hold on tight to each other
Screaming at the top of our lungs
This is my world
This is my world
I won't let you destroy it with your hate
Not today
Not tomorrow
Not ever
Even if I die trying
I promise you
Hate won't win
Not on my watch

Not
On
My
Watch

Sun Set, Moon Rise

As the sun sets
Brilliant colors streak the sky
Tears of a rainbow
Slipping behind the trees
Sliding into the sea
Taking dreams of sunlight
Into the night
Waves ripping apart today
As the wind carries promises of tomorrow
Reflected in the moon's rise

Chimes Keep Time

The chimes rang in the distance
Measuring my steps
One, two, three, four
As I walked through a forest of crumbling buildings
Taller than the trees
Blocking the minuscule light left
After the catastrophe
Ignoring facts to line pockets
Nothing left to fight over
My steps kept rhythm to the chimes
Five, six, seven, eight
Where were you when
Man created Armageddon
To fulfill a man-made prophecy
While lining the pockets of corporations
Now reduced to ruins in the aftermath
Of the dying population
Of the destroyed resources
Of a home where living is dying
The chimes mark the end of my journey
Nine, ten, eleven, twelve
The chimes fall silent
Greed destroyed us all

Earth's Vengeance

Dark, gloomy eyes stared out
From underneath falling tears
The world storming inside green irises
Looking toward hidden stars
Where everything seemed to drift toward oblivion
As the world changed without preamble
Violent floods raged stealing coastlines
Blizzards piled snow to the treetops
Rain pelted on ground it couldn't penetrate
Volcanoes spewed lava over cities and towns
Earthquakes split the ground to swallow stolen resources
The air stung lungs with every inhale and exhale
Leaves withered on dying trees
Flowers without nectar ceased blooming
She looked out at the barren horizon
A lone wolf left to tame the elements
As the Earth screamed her revenge
The atmosphere killing Earth's murderers
Leaving nothing in its wake
The wolf howls at a moon no longer visible
Wonders whether it's day or night
Lies down with one last exhale
Of acidic air
Her last thought
What were humans thinking?
Was greed and power worth the Earth?
Money and power sure as hell didn't save them
When Earth reached her breaking point
And struck back with a vengeance

Earth's Invoice to Us

Standing quiet
Eyes closed
Ears refusing to hear
Nose blocking the scents
Skin refusing to feel the wind
Mouth shut against the flavor of night
I let myself drift into one
With the Earth that sustains
Quietly sank to sit on dew dampened grass
Opened my eyes to see fireflies flitting by
Listened to frogs singing in the pond
Drew in the odor of fresh overturned soil
Savored the cool dry breeze blowing by
Tasted the flavor of nature on my tongue
Felt a tear slip down my cheek
As I felt the chemical stain of humans
Wrecking the Earth that sustains us
Pesticides, insecticides, herbicides
Fertilizers, antibiotics, hormones
Industrial waste, farm waste, mining waste
Air pollution, noise pollution, ground pollution
All infecting
The air we breathe
The food we eat
The water we drink
The breeze brushing our skin
The sounds surrounding us
We drown out all the Earth provides
In the name of greed
Wrapped up in packaging to make it acceptable
Progress, success, need

What we fail to admit is our sense of entitlement
For what we want is little more than an excuse
To plunder the Earth and leave its inhabitants
Worse off for our existence
Someday, somewhere, somehow
The bill will come due
The Earth will invoice us
And the cost will be so high
For the battle we're waging
Against our own best interests
To line the pockets of those who need nothing
While leaving those who need everything
And what will we do
When the Earth sends us that final invoice
The one money can't pay...

Written Between

Last night I looked up
Saw the writing between the stars
Never wanted to believe
Love couldn't solve everything
But, what can love do
When pollution obscures the sky
And water runs rusty
As I stood staring at the smoke
In the distance billowing from a smokestack
My body refused to inhale
My lungs refused to exhale
So I stood there
Seeing what was written
Between the greed and the hate
Where wars are more profitable than peace
And human beings are pawns in an unwinnable game
Democracy is for sale and the republic is already bought
So where does love fit into the script?
It's always love that saves the day in the movies
Yet, here we stand, with our weapon of love
Facing down a growing monster
That threatens our very existence
Suddenly all that love feels like a luxury
We can't afford
Yet, if you take away love
My hope will shrivel up and die
And that's not an option
So...
Even if love can't un-pollute the world
Even if love can't un-greed the world
Even if love can't un-war the world

Even if love can't un-corrupt a democratic republic
I'll cling to love like a life raft
In the middle of a raging sea
Because hate can't win
No matter how loud it roars through the night

Quiet Roar

The water below her trickled
It had once crashed onto the rocks below
But the drought had dried up the water
The water once so clear and pristine
Now a trickle of pollution sliding
Between the rocks instead of over them
She watched it in wonder
So much water now diverted to greed
Filling pockets and leaving people thirsty
Those in need silenced by those in power
She touched the water cautiously
Looked at the dying vegetation
What more could she do?
A tear trickled down her face
She listened for the rustle of wildlife
Heard nary a sound not even a bird chirping
At this point, she'd even welcome
The slither of a snake through the dry grass
But nothing
She looked up at the oil rig where once
Evergreens had filled the sky
She could no longer see
The snow-covered mountaintop in the distance
She trembled at the arrogance
That destroyed its own home
In the name of power and greed
But in the silence
She heard the roar building
The quiet roar of an Earth
That would have the final say

Uprooted

Roots pulling from the ground
As branches stretch for the sky
Seeking nourishment from sunlight
Seeking growth from new heights
Looking for survival
Seeking to thrive
Self-pruning all the dying material
The decay of dropped branches and leaves
Decomposing into fertilizer
Feeding the undergrowth on the forest floor
Roots tenting above the ground
Like hands in a yoga pose
Seeking one more inch of flexibility to push
The whole toward a better existence
While clinging to the forest floor
The foundation of old growth
Seeking new growth
In a forest that refuses to capitulate
To the forces of humanity's destruction

Pillar of Salt

You grabbed my hand
Pulled me forward
Ordered
"Don't look back."
As I started to turn
You pulled me forward
"I won't turn to a pillar of salt."
I spat the words at you
"You don't want to see it."
You whispered gently.
"That's not your decision to make."
You dropped my hand with a sigh.
I turned and looked
Collapsed to the ground in sobs
It was all gone
Everything I loved no longer existed
Suddenly I wished I *could* turn
To a pillar of salt
You placed a hand on my shoulder
I shook it off, dried my tears, and stood
I stepped in front of you
Marched forward
"Let's go."
I said through gritted teeth.
"I tried to warn you."
Your voice shook as you spoke.
"I needed to see."
I said quietly.
Then let out a bloodcurdling scream
That echoed back through the canyon walls
You sighed.

Without turning back, I spoke into the wind. "The future awaits."

Mother Earth Weeps

Mother Earth weeping
Human indifference felt
Life withers away

Dedicated to the Future

While I can imagine a million scenarios
I don't really know what you hold
Yet I know you will come
And I will embrace you
I know I will fight for love
I know I will fight for justice
I know I will fight for science
I will give you a fighting chance
To help me make life better for us all
I honor that time and again
You are there when it seems the world will end
And someday we'll face the moment
When you no longer exist
No one will be left to mourn you
No one will be left to honor you
No one will be left to embrace you
And what will that mean as the Earth heals herself
To start life all over again
Or perhaps disintegrates into a million pieces
Spread across the universe to start over again
In that sense I suppose you, future, are
The only thing that is immortal

Acknowledgments

My thanks to Loay Abu-Husein for helping elevate my cover design and make the technical details work.

Many documentaries, books, the work of many activists, and scientific research have inspired many of the poems in this book.

As always, I couldn't write without the support of my husband, Loay, my friends, and my family who have encouraged and inspired me all my life and continue to do so.

Other Books By T. L. Cooper

Poetry:

The Gift of Grief

Democracy in Silhouette

Vulnerability in Silhouette

Strength in Silhouette

Memory in Silhouette

Reflections in Silhouette

Love in Silhouette

Short Stories:

Take a Chance & Other Stories of Starting Over

Soaring Betrayal

Fiction:

All She Ever Wanted

About the Author

T. L. Cooper is the author of several books of poetry, two collections of short stories, and a novel. Her poems, short stories, articles, and essays have appeared online, in books, and in magazines. She grew up on a farm in Tollesboro, Kentucky. She currently lives in Albany, Oregon. When not writing, she enjoys yoga, meditating, creating plant-based recipes, and exploring the world.

www.ingramcontent.com/pod-product-compliance
Lightning Source LLC
Chambersburg PA
CBHW032058020426
42335CB00011B/397